This book was brought
to you by the
Naumes Family Foundation

STRIVING INTO 2000

By Stuart Kallen

Visit us at
www.abdopub.com

Published by ABDO Publishing Company, 4940 Viking Drive, Edina, MN 55435.
Copyright © 2001 by Abdo Consulting Group, Inc. International copyrights reserved in all countries. No part of this book may be reproduced in any form without written permission from the publisher.

Printed in the United States.

Edited by: Paul Joseph
Graphic Design: City Desktop Productions

Cover Photos: Corbis
Interior Photos: Corbis

Library of Congress Cataloging-in-Publication Data

Kallen, Stuart A., 1955 -
    Striving Into 2000 / Stuart Kallen
       p. cm. -- (Black History)
    Includes index.
    ISBN 1-57765-467-6
    1. Afro-Americans--History--1964--Juvenile literature. 2. Afro-Americans--Social conditions--1975--Juvenile literature. 3. Mandela, Nelson, 1918--Juvenile literature. 4. South Africa--Politics and government--1948-1994--Juvenile literature. [1. Afro-Americans. 2. Race relations. 3. Mandela, Nelson, 1918- 4. South Africa--Politics and government--1948-1994] I. Title

E185.615 .K27 2001
973'.0496073--dc21   00-056888

CONTENTS

Nelson Mandela gazing out his prison window.

Chapter 1—The Seventies 5

  Years of Violence 6

  A Prison Riot 7

  Busing 9

    Busing in Boston 9

  Affirmative Action 10

  Advances in the Seventies 13

    African-Americans In Politics 13

  The Freedom of Information Act 15

    Exposing Government Harassment 15

Chapter 2—The Eighties and Nineties 16
    Gains in the 1980s and 1990s 17

Timeline 20

Chapter 3—Black Leaders of Today 22
    Colin Powell (1937-) Military Leader and Secretary of State 22
    Jesse Jackson (1941-) Civil Rights Leader 24
    Toni Morrison (1931-) Novelist 26
    Tiger Woods (1975-) Professional Golfer 27
    Oprah Winfrey (1954-) Entertainment Executive 29

Chapter 4—Nelson Mandela and Apartheid 31
    Life in Johannesburg 32
    The Laws of Apartheid 33
    Mandela Reacts 34
        Mandela Is Arrested 35
        Mandela Goes Underground 36
    Free At Last! 39
    Mandela in America 40
    The End of Apartheid 41
    A Final Word 42
    Subject Map 43

Internet Sites 44

Glossary 45

Index 48

CHAPTER 1

THE SEVENTIES

As the 1970s began, the movement toward equality for all people seemed to be gathering speed. Thurgood Marshall, a black lawyer, was appointed to the U.S. Supreme Court in 1967. That same year, Carl Stokes was elected mayor of Cleveland, Ohio. He became the first black mayor of a large northern city. In the South, blacks were elected as mayors, city councilors, and sheriffs.

But other factors pointed to problems that lay ahead. Between

Supreme Court Justice Thurgood Marshall

1960 and 1970, over three million black people moved from rural areas to large cities. During these same years, over 2.5 million white people moved from large cities to the suburbs. This "white flight" resulted in fewer jobs and lower property values for the growing black population.

Years of Violence

The late sixties and early seventies were marred by violence in many cities. After the death of Martin Luther King, Jr., in 1968, major riots erupted in dozens of cities. Hundreds of people were killed or wounded. Fires and looting caused millions of dollars in damage. Some people

Bullet holes riddle the window of a women's dormitory at Jackson State College in Mississippi. Police fired into the dormitory killing two and wounding 12 students of the historically black college.

felt that nonviolent methods could no longer be effective in ending discrimination. Anger and frustration continued to build. Cities went up in flames.

On May 14, 1970, a demonstration was held at Jackson State College in Mississippi. Two black students were killed and 12 were wounded. The students were protesting the American invasion of Cambodia. They were also protesting the killing of four white students at Kent State University 10 days earlier. Whereas the Kent State deaths created a national uproar, the Jackson State killings of blacks received less attention.

A Prison Riot

On September 9, 1971, hundreds of black inmates took over the state prison in Attica, New York. The prisoners demanded better living conditions, food, and schooling. For four days, the prisoners held several guards as hostages. Tensions mounted as food supplies ran low. Hundreds of New York State troopers surrounded the prison. Police helicopters circled overhead.

A crowd of inmates with fists raised— Attica, New York

New York Governor Nelson Rockefeller

Specialists talked to the prisoners and listened to their demands. After the negotiators agreed to help the prisoners, they left the prison. Then Governor Nelson Rockefeller ordered the police to attack. Fifteen hundred state troopers stormed the prison. They opened fire on the inmates. Thirty-three inmates were killed. Ten guards who had been hostages were also killed. An investigation showed that many of the prisoners were shot while trying to surrender. After the uprising, conditions at the prison got even worse.

Damaged furniture and debris in prison hallway.

Busing

The government had ordered schools to integrate in 1955. But in 1970, there were still hundreds of American schools that had only black students. In many of these schools, there were shortages of basic items such as books and pencils. The schools for black students were often old, decaying buildings in inner-city neighborhoods. Once again, black parents who wanted better education for their children looked to the courts for help.

In 1971, the Supreme Court ordered schools to use school buses to achieve integration. White students were bused to black schools. Black students were bused to white schools. Like every other decision to integrate, this one met with great resistance. In 1972, President Nixon asked Congress to put a stop to busing. Congress refused. Busing became federal policy despite Nixon's objections.

Busing in Boston

In 1974, Federal Judge Arthur Garrity ruled that the city of Boston, Massachusetts, must bus 17,000 students to achieve racial equality. Garrity said that Boston's black schools were "the most crowded, the oldest, the least maintained, and the most poorly staffed."

When school started at South Boston High in September 1974, 90 percent of the white students stayed home. Black students who were bused in from Roxbury were pelted with stones. Rocks shattered the windows of the buses. For weeks, white parents surrounded the high schools and screamed insults at black students. Inside the schools, there were many fights every day between black and white students.

In mid-October, a black student at Boston's Hyde Park High School stabbed a white student. Over 450 National Guardsmen were called out to stop the riot that followed. In December, a white mob trapped 135 black students inside South Boston High. Thousands of white adults surrounded the school. The mob threatened the lives of

the black students for four hours. School buses parked at the school's front door to fool the mob. The mob showered the volunteer bus drivers with stones. Meanwhile, the black students sneaked out the school's back door.

School officials ordered an early Christmas vacation. The vacation lasted for an entire month. When 31 black students returned to school in January, they were protected by 500 police officers. By 1976, over 20,000 white students had fled Boston's public schools. Most of them went to private schools or moved from the city.

Anti-busing rally in south Boston.

Affirmative Action

Affirmative action programs are a way to offer opportunities to members of minority groups. These programs aim to give certain groups advantages that they were denied in the past. Such programs give preference to minorities and women in job hiring and school admissions. President John F. Kennedy first coined the phrase "affirmative action" in 1961. Kennedy wanted companies with government contracts to hire more black people. In 1965, President Lyndon Johnson signed an executive order. This order said that companies must hire a certain percentage of black workers, depending on how many blacks lived in the area. The Supreme

Court supported affirmative action. Large companies that did not follow the rules were fined.

Many business owners were opposed to these policies. They thought that the government was unfairly interfering with their business. They did not want to be told who to hire and who to promote. Also, some white students were angered by "reverse discrimination." They argued that black students had an unfair advantage, due to the fact that openings were set aside in schools for them. Some white workers felt that unqualified blacks were being promoted because of their skin color. On the other hand, many people supported affirmative action. They felt these programs could help to reverse 350 years of slavery and discrimination.

President Lyndon B. Johnson

In 1978, the medical school at UC-Davis turned down Allan

Bakke, a white Vietnam veteran. This school had a policy of affirmative action. Sixteen openings in the medical school were reserved for blacks, Hispanics, and other minorities. Bakke's grades and test scores were better than some of these students'.

Vietnam veteran Allan Bakke

For four years, Bakke fought affirmative action in the courts. As the case dragged on, a number of questions came to the surface. How should the government help people who have faced racism for hundreds of years? At what cost? The Civil Rights Act of 1965 guaranteed equal rights to all people. Does this apply to whites who cannot attend college or find a job because of racial quotas? Do white people have an advantage because of better

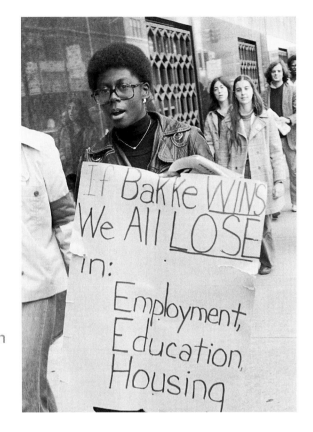

Protesters in Detroit, Michigan

schools and more opportunities? Hundreds of groups argued on one side or another. Finally, the court ruled to admit Bakke to Davis. This decision weakened affirmative action programs. Little by little, the policy was chipped away.

   In the summer of 1989, the Supreme Court heard three cases about these matters. Each time, they decided to place limits on affirmative action. In one case, white firefighters in Alabama argued that they were victims of reverse discrimination. The Supreme Court agreed. After the ruling, many employers began to abandon affirmative action. In the 1990s, the Court continued to restrict such programs. In a 1995 case, the Court stated that such programs are unconstitutional, unless they fulfill "a compelling government interest."

Advances in the Seventies

African-Americans in Politics

The protests, marches, and sit-ins of the 1960s began to pay off in the 1970s. Voters elected more black people to public office than ever before.

In 1972, Shirley Chisholm became the first black woman to run for president. Also in 1972, Georgia's Andrew Young was elected to Congress. Young was the first black congressman to come from the Deep South in 70 years. Two black women were also elected to Congress for the first time in 1972. Barbara Jordan from Texas was elected to the House of Representatives. So was Yvonne Burke from California. Also, Senator Edward Brooke of Massachusetts was re-elected. In 1966, he had become the first black to be elected to the Senate since Reconstruction.

Shirley Chisholm was elected to Congress in 1968 and was the first African-American woman to serve as a U.S. Representative.

In addition, three men were elected mayors of major American cities in 1973. Thomas Bradley was elected in Los Angeles. Maynard Jackson was elected in Atlanta. And Coleman Young became the mayor of Detroit.

President Jimmy Carter

In 1976, Jimmy Carter, the governor of Georgia, was elected president. When he was governor, Carter was very popular with black voters. He also appointed many black advisors. As president, Carter named Patricia Harris to be his Secretary of Housing and Urban Development (HUD). Harris was the first black woman to become a Cabinet officer. In 1978, she became Secretary of Health, Education, and Welfare. Carter also named Andrew Young as Ambassador to the United Nations. Young spoke out against racism in Africa and other parts of the world.

Patricia Harris

Andrew Young

The Freedom of Information Act

Exposing Government Harassment

Another law that helped black people in the 1970s was the Freedom of Information Act (FOIA). This law was passed in 1966. Over time, it led to the release of secret documents from the FBI and other government agencies. Some of these documents told of the FBI harassment of black groups in the 1960s. For years, the FBI had sought to discredit Martin Luther King, Jr., and his civil rights groups. The FBI also worked to "neutralize" black groups like the Black Panthers and Black Muslims. This new knowledge led to stricter controls of the FBI's domestic spy programs.

CHAPTER 2

THE EIGHTIES AND NINETIES

As the 1980s began, black people faced new and complex problems. The American economy was weak. This caused a huge rise in unemployment. The prices of most products rose quickly. Government programs that helped black people began to meet resistance from voters and politicians. As more people competed for fewer jobs, programs like affirmative action came under attack.

During the 1960s, the black struggle was one of the main focuses of the national media. During the 1980s, the struggle for civil rights widened. Many other groups began to use the language of the equal rights movement. These groups included Hispanics, women, the disabled, and the elderly.

President Ronald Reagan

But while more and more groups strove for equality, there was less money to go around. This caused the movement toward equality to slow down.

Republican Ronald Reagan was elected president on November 4, 1980. In his inaugural address, Reagan said, "Government is the problem, not the solution." The federal government cut taxes and spending on social programs. Reagan's programs helped to bring inflation under control. But they did not help to close the wide gap between the rich and the poor. Many of these poor were blacks. In 1990, one out of every three black households earned less than $10,000 per year. Fewer than one out of seven white households fell into this category.

Gains in the 1980s and 1990s

Blacks also made many gains during the 1980s. Between the Voting Rights Act of 1965 and the end of the 1980s, the number of registered black voters doubled. In 1965, less than 100 blacks held elective offices. In 1989, more than 6,800 blacks held office. That number included 24 congressmen and 300 mayors. The most dramatic changes came in Mississippi. In the late 1980s, that state led the nation in the number of black officials.

David Dinkins

In 1990, David Dinkins became the first black mayor of New York City. Also in 1990, Douglas Wilder of Virginia became the first black governor in American history.

By 1990, the days of fighting for integrated schools in the South seemed like ancient history. All across the South, black and white children began to attend the same schools. In 1960, there were 281,000 black college graduates in the United States. By the early 1990s, that number leaped to over two million.

In the business world, over 200,000 black men and women became corporate managers in the 1980s. In many fields, blacks found it difficult to rise to the top. But companies could no longer ignore the talent and drive of black executives.

George Bush was elected President of the United States in 1988. In his first

President George Bush

months in office, Bush named Dr. Louis Sullivan as the Secretary of Health and Human Services. Sullivan sought to improve health care for America's poor. Bush also named several blacks to important departments in his Cabinet. His wife, Barbara, hired Anna Perez to be her press secretary. Perez became the first black woman to act as press secretary for a first lady.

In 1992, Bill Clinton was elected to the presidency. That same year, Carol Moseley Braun of Illinois ran for the Senate. Moseley Braun was a graduate of the University of Chicago Law School. She had also served in the Illinois State Congress for 10 years. Though her campaign did not have a lot of money, Moseley Braun upset her opponents and

President Bill Clinton

won the election. She became the first black woman ever elected to the U.S. Senate. In 1998, Moseley Braun lost her bid for reelection. She was named U.S. Ambassador to New Zealand in 1999.

Carol Mosley Braun

TIMELINE

1948 "Apartheid" laws passed in South Africa

1956 Nelson Mandela is arrested for protesting Apartheid

1960 Sixty-nine people are killed when police fire into a crowd of protesters in Sharpeville, South Africa

1961 Mandela is found guilty and temporarily released; he goes into hiding

1962 Mandela is captured and put in prison

1965 President Johnson signs an executive order implementing affirmative action

1966 Congress passes the Freedom of Information Act

1967 Thurgood Marshall is appointed to the U.S. Supreme Court

1970 Two black students are killed by police during a demonstration at Jackson State College in Mississippi

1971 Supreme Court orders mandatory busing to integrate public schools

———— Attica prison riot

1972 Shirley Chisholm becomes the first black woman to run for President, and Texan Barbara Jordan and Californian Yvonne Burke become the first black women elected to the House of Representatives

1974 Busing is ordered in Boston; many whites violently oppose it

1989 General Colin Powell becomes Chairman of the Joint Chiefs of Staff

1990 Nelson Mandela is freed from prison by South African President F.W. de Klerk

———— Douglas Wilder of Virginia becomes the first black Governor

1992 Carol Moseley-Braun becomes the first black woman elected to the U.S. Senate

1993 Toni Morrison becomes the first black woman to win Nobel Prize for Literature

———— Mandela and de Klerk win the Nobel Peace Prize for their work to end Apartheid

1996 Mandela is elected President of South Africa

2001 Colin Powell becomes Secretary of State

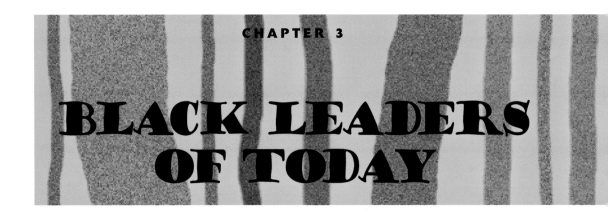

CHAPTER 3

BLACK LEADERS OF TODAY

Colin Powell (1937–)

Military Leader and Secretary of State

Colin Powell was born in Harlem on April 5, 1937. His parents were Jamaican immigrants. They taught Colin to place a high value on education. After high school, he enrolled at the City College of New York. There he studied geology. He also joined the Reserve Officers Training Corps (ROTC). This was Powell's first exposure to the military. He became commander of his drill unit. In 1958, he graduated at the top of his ROTC class.

After graduation, Powell became a second lieutenant in the U.S. Army. President Kennedy sent him to South Vietnam in 1962. The next year, he was wounded by a trap while on patrol. He was awarded the Purple Heart and the Bronze Star for his service.

In 1968, Powell returned to Vietnam. This time, he was injured in a helicopter crash. Despite being hurt, Powell rescued several other men from the burning wreck. He earned the Soldiers Medal for his brave actions. In 1972, he was awarded the Legion of Merit.

After he returned from Vietnam, Powell earned a master's degree in business. He served in the federal government under Presidents

Nixon, Ford, Carter, and Reagan. Then, early in 1989, he was named head of the Armed Forces Command. Later that year Powell became a four-star general.

In August of 1989, President Bush appointed Powell chairman of the Joint Chiefs of Staff. He was the first black person ever to serve in this position. In 1990 and 1991, Powell led Operations Desert Shield and Storm. These successful campaigns pushed the Iraqi army out of Kuwait. They also made Powell a famous national figure.

After the Gulf War, Powell retired from the military. Many people urged Powell to run for president in 1996. Because of his bravery, intelligence, and popularity, many thought that he could become the first black president. But Powell declined to run. Instead in 2001, he was appointed Secretary of State by President George W. Bush. Powell was the first black person to serve in this position. After president, it is believed to be the most important job in the United States.

Throughout his career, people of all colors have admired Colin Powell's dignity and dedication to his country.

Chairman of the Joint Chiefs of Staff, Colin Powell

Jesse Jackson (1941–)

Civil Rights Leader

Jesse Jackson was born in Greenville, South Carolina, in 1941. He starred in several sports at Sterling High School. After graduation, Jackson earned a football scholarship to the University of Illinois. There, he learned that blacks could not play quarterback on the football team. Jackson decided to transfer to North Carolina A&T in Greensboro.

While in Greensboro, Jackson became involved in the civil rights movement. In 1963, he led a sit-in that lasted 10 months. The protest was a success. It helped to integrate the public facilities of Greensboro. In 1965, Jackson went to Selma, Alabama to march with Dr. Martin Luther King, Jr. After they met, Jackson became a member of King's staff.

In 1966, Jackson moved to Chicago. There he attended a theological seminary. He also continued to work for equal rights. In Chicago, Jackson helped to found a branch of Dr. King's Operation Breadbasket. The goal of this project was to expand the job market for blacks. In 1967, Jackson became the

The Reverend Jesse Jackson

national leader of this project. He began boycotts of companies that discriminated against black people. As a result, many companies began to hire more blacks. Many white-owned companies also began to work with businesses owned by blacks.

In 1968, Jackson became a Baptist minister. In 1971, he founded Operation PUSH. PUSH stands for People United to Save Humanity. This program sought to improve the economic and political status of minority groups. PUSH sought to make more people aware of the problems of racism. It challenged big companies to be fair in their hiring and contracting. The operation was a success. PUSH branches were set up in several cities. In 1976, Jackson began PUSH for Excellence. This program helped black students to attend college.

Jackson knew that politics could be a vital tool for improving the status of blacks. He began touring the country to urge blacks to vote. He also became interested in world affairs. He traveled the globe, and tried to help resolve disputes between nations. In 1979, he went to the Middle East to meet with the leaders of Israel, Lebanon, Syria, Egypt, and Palestine. Unfortunately, his peace talks did little to solve the problems in that part of the world.

In the 1980s, Jackson became the top spokesman for black Americans. In 1983, Harold Washington became the first black mayor of Chicago. Jackson's work to register voters was vital to this achievement. In 1984, Jackson ran for president. He was not the first black candidate, but he was the first to gain wide support. Jackson did not win the Democratic nomination, but he received the majority of the black vote.

To gain white voter support, Jackson began the Rainbow Coalition. This group addressed the needs of women, the poor, Hispanics, and other voters who felt that their needs were being ignored.

In 1988, Jackson ran for president again. Like before, he did not receive his party's nomination. But his fiery speeches focused new attention on the problems of minorities. In 1990, Jackson became a "statehood senator" from the District of Columbia. It was his first elected office.

From the sit-ins in the South to presidential politics, Jesse Jackson proved that black people are ready to lead America. He has helped to carry the ideals of the 1960s into modern America. Jesse Jackson keeps the dream alive.

Toni Morrison (1931–)

Novelist

Toni Morrison's original name was Chloe Wofford. She was born on February 18, 1931, in Lorain, Ohio. When Morrison was growing up, her family had a deep love of black culture. Stories, songs, and folk tales became important parts of her childhood. She attended Howard

and Cornell Universities. She excelled in writing at both schools.

After college, Morrison worked as a teacher and a fiction editor. In 1958, she married an architect named

Toni Morrison

Harold Morrison. They had two sons before they divorced. In 1970, she published her first book, *The Bluest Eye.* It was about a young black girl named Pecola. Pecola becomes obsessed with white ideas of beauty. She longs to have blue eyes, as the pretty white girls do. Since, then Morrison has published six more novels. *Beloved,* published in 1987, won the Pulitzer Prize for fiction. In 1987, Morrison became Professor of Humanities at Princeton University. Along with her teaching and writing, she works for the conservation of black American culture.

The main theme of all of Morrison's books is the experience of black people in America. Her characters are both men and women. They come from different backgrounds and live in different eras. But all struggle with the question of what it means to be a black American. Toni Morrison's novels are admired all over the world. In 1993, she became the first black woman to win the Nobel Prize for Literature.

Tiger Woods (1975–)

Professional Golfer

Eldrick "Tiger" Woods was born in Cypress, California on December 30, 1975. Woods' father Earl, nicknamed his son "Tiger" after his friend. Tiger was still sleeping in a crib when he began to show interest in the game of golf. At six months old, Tiger would imitate his father as he hit balls into a practice net. Within two years he was on television putting with Bob Hope. Tiger joined his father on the golf course as soon as he could walk. He could keep his golf score before he could count to five. At five years old, he was featured in *Golf Digest.*

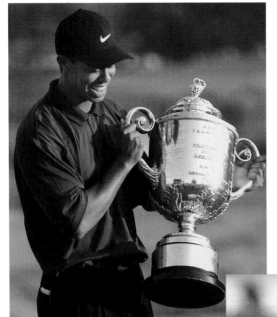

Top photo: Tiger Woods holding the Wanamaker trophy after winning the PGA Championship.

Bottom photo: Tiger Woods watches his shot to the first green during the World Golf Championships 2000 NEC Invitational.

Woods' competitive nature surfaced in grade school. He won the Optimist International Junior tournament at eight years old. He won it five more times before he could drive a car. At 15, he became the youngest golfer to win the U.S. Junior Amateur. He won two more U.S. Junior Amateur titles in a row. At the age of 18, he became the youngest golfer to win the U.S. Amateur. Woods entered Stanford University as a freshman in 1994. He remained there for two years and continued to win tournaments. He collected six USGA Amateur titles from 1991 to 1996 and many player-of-the-year awards.

Woods turned pro after his third straight U.S. Amateur title in August of 1996. In 1997, he became the youngest Masters champion ever. He was the first player of black heritage to win a major golf tournament. In 2000, he became the youngest golfer to win the career grand slam.

Woods has become one of the most recognizable sports figures in the world. He is a spokesman for Nike, Wheaties, and Buick. He has created charities to make golf and higher education available to disadvantaged kids. He has been considered by many to be the best golfer of all time.

Oprah Winfrey (1954–)

Entertainment Executive Oprah Winfrey was born January 29, 1954, in the small town of Kosciusko, Mississippi. When she was young, Oprah lived on a farm with her grandmother. She was reading to anyone who would listen by age three. At six years old, Winfrey moved to Milwaukee with her mother. There she was abused

Oprah Winfrey

and ran away from home. She was sent to a juvenile center when she was 13, but it was full. Instead, they moved her to Nashville, Tennessee, to live with her father. He was a strict man. He made sure that Oprah was always home on time. She also had to read a book each week and give him a report on it. This helped Oprah prepare for her future.

In high school, Winfrey started her broadcast career at WVOL radio in Nashville. She later went to Tennessee State University. She studied Speech Communications and Performing Arts. She left radio at age 19 to become WTVF's youngest television anchor. This also made her the first African-American news anchor at the station. In 1976, Winfrey moved to Baltimore. She was a co-anchor and reporter on WJZ-TV news. Within two years, she was co-host of the show *People Are Talking.*

In 1984, she moved to Chicago to host a morning talk show called *AM Chicago.* It quickly became the hottest show in Chicago. In September 1985, the name of the show was changed to *The Oprah Winfrey Show.* It was a national talk show by 1986. Oprah started HARPO Productions, Inc. in 1986 and later purchased her show from ABC in 1988. This made Winfrey the first woman to own and produce her own talk show. *The Oprah Winfrey Show* was the number one talk show from 1986 through 1999.

The success of her talk show has helped Oprah to influence other groups. In 1991, she spoke to Congress in support of the National Child Protection Act. Her goal was to create a national database of convicted child abusers. It became law in 1993. "Oprah's Angel Network," has raised over $3.5 million in scholarships. Through HARPO Films, Winfrey makes movies for ABC and Walt Disney. She bought part of a cable and internet company called Oxygen Media in 1998. She started teaching at Northwestern University in 1999 and published her first magazine in 2000. All of this put Winfrey on *Time Magazine*'s list of the 100 most influential people of the 20th century.

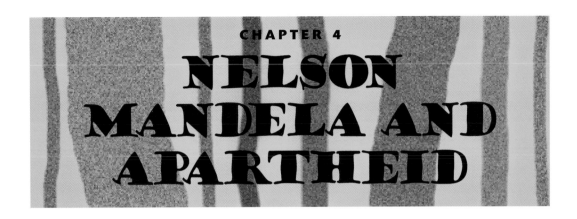

CHAPTER 4

NELSON MANDELA AND APARTHEID

When Nelson Mandela was a young boy, he loved to listen to the stories of the tribal elders. As the fire burned into the night, the elders would talk about life in Africa before white men from Europe arrived. "Our people lived peacefully, under the democratic rule of the kings," Mandela later said. "We moved freely up and down the country without hindrance. The country was ours . . . we occupied the land, the forests, the rivers . . . We set up and operated our own government, we controlled our own armies, and we organized our own trade and commerce."

Nelson Mandela in tribal clothes.

By the time Mandela was born on July 18, 1918, those days were just a memory. Mandela grew up in a world where white Europeans ruled his country. But those stories of the old days inspired him to devote his life to the rights of his people. His tribal name, Rolihlahla, pointed the way to Nelson's future. It means "stirring up trouble."

Mandela's father was a tribal chief. He taught young Nelson about the British and Dutch settlers who came to South Africa with guns. The Europeans forced the blacks to be slaves. They also brought people from India to work as slaves. In 1910, the British government gave one million white South Africans, known as Afrikaners, control over 4.5 million "nonwhites." The Afrikaners passed laws to restrict the movements of the blacks. They could not move freely in their own country. The laws were enforced with clubs and guns. When Mandela was young, he heard the history of "rivers running red with African blood."

In 1930, when Mandela was 12-years-old, his father died. Nelson went to a Methodist boarding school. There he practiced traditional tribal customs. He also earned a Bachelor of Arts degree. Mandela's studies were cut short when he was suspended for taking part in a student strike.

Life in Johannesburg

When Mandela was 22-years-old, he moved to the noisy, fast-paced city of Johannesburg. The train he rode was marked by a sign that said "for Non-Europeans." In Johannesburg, Mandela found that the buses, restaurants, cafes, and public restrooms were labeled "Europeans Only." Even the park benches carried this label. Mandela did not see much of the white part of town. Soon he was in one of the "native" locations.

In the black section of town, there was no electricity, telephones, sewers, or plumbing. The police often raided the area, looking for blacks without "passes." Like all blacks in the city, Mandela needed a pass to get a job, live in a town, travel, and be out after the 11 p.m. curfew. Without a pass, he would be arrested.

Mandela found work as a lawyer in an all-white firm. He married his first wife, Ntoko Mase. They moved to a part of the city known as Soweto. There, Mandela became involved with the African National Congress (ANC). Four African lawyers who were trained in Britain and America founded the ANC in 1912. The ANC wanted to unite the African people against the European repression.

Nelson Mandela in his law office in Johannesburg, South Africa in 1952.

The Laws of Apartheid

In 1948, the Afrikaner National Party came to power in South Africa. This party passed a series of laws known as apartheid. The policy of apartheid classified each person according to race or tribe. There were three main groups. These were Bantu (all black Africans), Coloured (mixed race) and white. Later, a fourth group, Asian, was added. The towns and rural areas of South Africa were divided into zones. In each zone, only one race could live and own property. All the best areas were set aside for white people. In all, 80 percent of the land was set aside for whites.

The government closed all schools and universities to nonwhites. It then set up schools for nonwhites that taught such activities as "tree planting" and "sheep herding."

Apartheid created laws that segregated every aspect of South African life. It created townships where nonwhites had to live. These townships were outside big cities where cheap labor was needed. Women had to carry passes. Blacks who were not needed for labor were sent to homelands. Usually, a man working in the city could not have his wife and children live with him in the township. Rather, the family had to live hundreds of miles away in the homeland. Because of this, families were separated for most of the year.

A law called the Suppression of Communism Act of 1951 stopped all forms of protest against apartheid. This law made it illegal to oppose the government. Books were banned and newspapers were censored. Free speech was stopped. Political meetings were outlawed.

Mandela Reacts

The apartheid laws alarmed Mandela and the ANC. In 1949, Mandela organized thousands of people to resist apartheid peacefully. Mandela toured the country giving speeches and organizing people. But the laws of apartheid made travel difficult. Sometimes Mandela had to walk miles and sleep under the nearest tree.

Protests began all over South Africa. Some blacks marched into "European Only" areas. Some refused to carry passes. Over 8,500 blacks were arrested. The government reacted by making stricter laws. The membership of the ANC climbed from 7,000 to 100,000 people. Mandela was put on trial and sentenced to nine months in prison. The government then outlawed political leaders like Mandela.

Although Mandela did not want to be a leader, he was elected president of the Johannesburg ANC. His charisma and electrifying speeches made him a born leader. Before he could take over leadership, the government banned him. Because he was banned, Mandela could not leave Johannesburg, attend meetings, or meet with more than one other person at a time. But Mandela continued to practice law, raise his three sons, and work for the ANC in secret.

Mandela Is Arrested

At dawn on December 5, 1956, Mandela and many others were arrested for violating the Suppression of Communism Act. Mandela did not consider himself a Communist. Still, the government used the act to charge Mandela. When the trial started, protesters gathered around the courthouse. They sang freedom songs. Eventually, Mandela was released on bail.

For the next five years, Mandela fought for his survival in court. He worked part time as a lawyer, but the trial put a strain on his marriage. Eventually Mandela and his wife divorced. In 1958, he met and married Nomzano Winifred (Winnie Mandela). They had two daughters.

In March 1960, after Mandela had been on trial for over four years, a protest was held in Sharpeville Township. The police fired into a crowd. Sixty-nine people were killed and 200 were wounded. Some of the victims were children. Horror and rage swept through the country. All over South Africa there were riots, strikes, and protest marches in the streets.

The South African government declared a state of emergency. The ANC was banned. Mandela was imprisoned. But during his trial, Mandela had impressed American and British observers. The ANC cause became known in Europe and America.

Students dressed as South African policemen re-enact shooting into Trafalgar Square on the anniversary of the Sharpeville Massacre.

On March 29, 1961, Mandela was found guilty. He was temporarily released. When he left the courtroom, he was carried on the shoulders of a cheering, dancing crowd.

Mandela Goes Underground

After the trial, Mandela returned to his home and told Winnie, "Darling, just pack a few of my clothes in a suitcase. I'm going away for a long time." Wearing a long coat and a hat pulled down over his face, Mandela went underground. He took over leadership of the ANC. He organized strikes and protests while on the run. It was hard for such a well-known man to hide, and he had some narrow escapes. One time he had to slide down a rope from a second-story apartment to escape the police as they came up the stairs. His daring escapes made him a legend in the African community.

During his period on the run, Mandela decided that sabotage was the only way to fight apartheid. Mandela formed the Spear of the

Nation. This group began to blow up telegraph lines. They destroyed government property, but vowed never to kill human beings. Mandela traveled to London and Algeria to speak to political leaders. He was thrilled when he saw blacks and whites working, shopping, and living together. When he returned to South Africa on August 5, 1962, Mandela was captured. Three police cars cornered him as he drove down a road near Durban. He had been underground for 17 months.

Mandela was sentenced to five years in prison. While in prison, he was put on trial for the sabotage he had done while underground. This time he was sentenced to life in prison.

Mandela was taken to Robben Island Prison. This prison sits on a cold, damp island near Cape Town. He was given a short-sleeve shirt and a pair of short pants. The clothes did not protect him from the bitter cold. The prison food was corn mush and coffee. Mandela spent years breaking rocks in the prison limestone quarry. Every six months he was allowed to write and receive one letter and visit one person for 30 minutes. During this period, Mandela lost 50 pounds. When Winnie came to visit, they were only able to see each other through a small glass window. They talked through a telephone. Mandela was not allowed to write a diary or see a newspaper.

Aerial view of Robbens Island where Nelson Mandela was imprisoned for 26 years.

Meanwhile, Winnie was put in prison for her work with the ANC. She was tortured and spent five months in solitary confinement. After spending another 10 months in jail, she was released. She had never been charged with a crime. When Winnie returned home, she was placed under house arrest. She couldn't leave home at nights or on weekends. After two years without a visit, Winnie was finally able to see her husband—for 30 minutes.

Winnie Mandela looks out from behind the barred gate at her home, where she lived in defiance of a government order.

In prison, Mandela organized hunger strikes to protest the poor living conditions. Because of worldwide pressure on the South African government, Mandela began to gain a few more freedoms while in prison. More frequent visits were allowed. Mandela was allowed to see his daughters, who were now teenagers.

Mandela was transferred to Pollsmore Prison in 1976. After 10 years there, the authorities tried to tempt him with offers of release. "Leave the country," they said. "Stop your political organizing," they said. He turned them all down. The government feared national riots if Mandela died in prison. They moved him to a prison where he had a swimming pool, telephone, and computers. The jailers started calling him Mr. Mandela.

Free At Last!

On February 5, 1990, South African's President F. W. de Klerk, lifted the 30 year ban on the ANC. He agreed to release 120 political prisoners. On February 11, Nelson Mandela walked out of prison into the waiting arms of Winnie—and the African people. Mandela was 71. He had spent 27 years in prison. Grey-haired and thin, Mandela returned to Cape Town. There he gave a rousing speech to thousands of cheering Africans. Mandela made it clear that time had not changed his goals—equal rights for South Africa's black population.

South African police use horsewhips on marchers headed for Pollsmoore Prison in support of political prisoner Nelson Mandela.

In the United States, millions of people, black and white, cheered the release of Mandela. But in South Africa, 15,000 whites marched through the streets chanting, "Hang Mandela!" Other black political parties disagreed with Mandela's positions and did not consider him their leader. But the first steps to a desegregated South Africa had been made.

White South Africans with the Conservative Party demonstrate against the release of Nelson Mandela from prison.

Mandela in America

In June 1990, Nelson Mandela traveled to the United States. In New York, he rode through the streets in a huge ticker-tape parade. Mayor David Dinkins gave him a key to the city. In his speeches, Mandela used the words of black American heroes like Martin Luther King, Jr., Malcolm X, and Marcus Garvey. Americans cheered as Mandela yelled, "Death to racism!"

From New York, Mandela made a cross-country tour. He spoke before the Congress and Senate. There he received several standing ovations. Mandela spoke with President Bush and asked for America's help in the South African struggle. American blacks treated Mandela like a hero everywhere he went.

Nelson Mandela stands with his wife, Winnie, and holds a gold key to the city of New York, which was presented to him by Mayor David Dinkins.

The End of Apartheid

After Mandela was released, he and President de Klerk worked together to end apartheid. In 1993, they shared the Nobel Peace Prize for their efforts. In April of 1994, South Africa held its first open elections. Mandela and the ANC won. He became President of South Africa. As president, Mandela worked hard to improve the living standards of black South Africans. In 1996, the country enacted a new constitution. In 1999, at the age of 81, Mandela retired. From his early protest work, to his faith and endurance during his many years in prison, to his work as president, Nelson Mandela has been one of the world's most inspiring leaders.

Secretary of State Colin Powell (left) with President George W. Bush.

A Final Word

Slavery ended over 130 years ago. Yet black people still struggle for equality and acceptance. But as the century ends and a new one begins, many black people have brighter futures than ever before. When Colin Powell was appointed Secretary of State by President George W. Bush in 2001 he took over one of the most important jobs in the world.

As new technology makes the world seem smaller, the fight against racism has spread all over the globe. In Africa, Europe, China, and other places, people are demanding equal rights and freedom. Often they use the techniques that American blacks developed during the 1960s.

As we enter a new millennium, we now know that all people have similar dreams and desires, no matter what color they are. People of all nations and ethnicities must join forces to fight environmental problems, war, racism, and hunger.

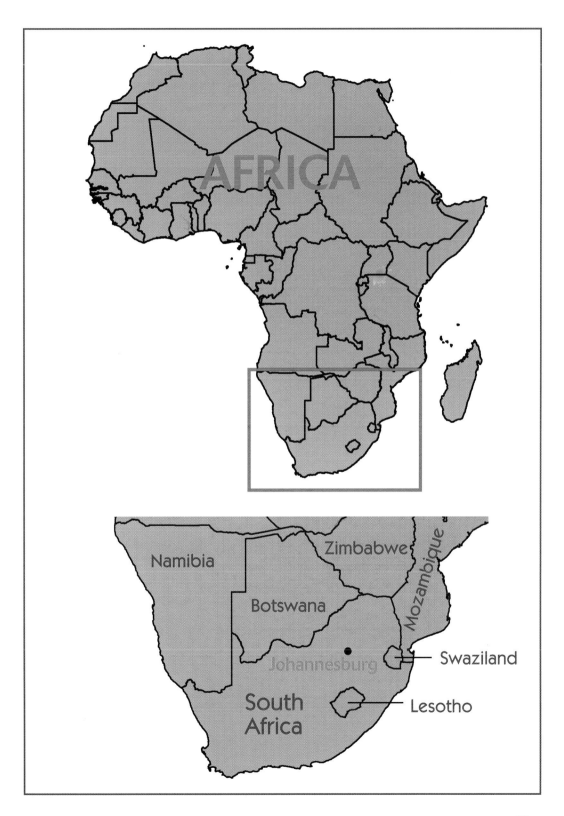

AFRICA

Namibia

Zimbabwe

Mozambique

Botswana

Johannesburg

Swaziland

South
Africa

Lesotho

43

INTERNET SITES

Apartheid—The Beginning

http://www.learner.org/exhibits/southafrica/apartheid.html

Read about the history of South Africa and Apartheid and test your knowledge with an interactive timeline.

Frontline: The Long Walk of Nelson Mandela

http://www.pbs.org/wgbh/pages/frontline/shows/mandela/etc/cron.html

See Nelson Mandela's life unfold from the confines of Apartheid to the Presidency of his country.

The FBI Freedom of Information Act Reading Room

http://foia.fbi.gov/

The official site to read the FBI's most requested files. This site is run as part of the federal act making formerly secret documents accessible to the public. Read up on the government's domestic spy programs and see how they monitored activists like Dr. Martin Luther King, Jr.

GLOSSARY

Affirmative Action—A government program that required companies to hire a certain percentage of black workers, depending on the number of blacks that lived in the area. Public colleges and universities were also required to set aside a number of spaces for black students.

African National Congress—Political party in South Africa founded in 1912 by four African lawyers. The ANC, as it is known, wanted to unite the African people against the European repression. Nelson Mandela was the most well-known leader of the ANC.

Afrikaners—Term for white South Africans.

Apartheid—A series of laws passed in 1948 by the ruling Europeans of South Africa that sought to keep the nonwhites separate from the whites. The laws kept nonwhites from attending schools and universities, and designated certain areas where they could live and work. Apartheid laws segregated every aspect of South African life.

Attica—New York State prison where hundreds of black inmates rioted and took control demanding better living conditions. After several days of negotiations, the Governor of New York ordered the police to attack resulting in the death of 33 inmates and 10 guards.

Busing—The Supreme Court ordered the busing of white students to black schools and black students to white schools to achieve integration and racial equality. In Boston, this policy met with violent opposition from white parents and students, and many chose to abandon public schooling rather than be bused to another school.

Freedom of Information Act—Law passed in 1966 that released government documents for public use. Some of the documents told of the FBI harassment of black groups in the 1960s such as the Black Panthers and the Black Muslims.

Nobel Prize—Award usually given annually for the encouragement of men and women who work for the interest of humanity. The award is given in several areas including peace, literature, science, and medicine.

Operation PUSH—PUSH (People United to Save Humanity) was a program founded by Jesse Jackson that sought to improve the status of minority groups and make people aware of the problems of racism.

Pulitzer Prize—Prestigious award for outstanding literary or journalistic achievement.

Rainbow Coalition—Political group founded by Jesse Jackson that addressed the needs of women, Hispanics, the poor, and other voters who felt they were being ignored.

Reconstruction—Shortly after the civil war, the Reconstruction Act of 1867 put southern states under military law to enforce the rights of newly freed blacks. The 14th and 15th amendments to the Constitution were passed during Reconstruction, giving equal rights to all races, and guaranteeing black men the right to vote. Federal troops left the south in 1877 marking the end of Reconstruction. Many blacks were elected to public office during this period.

Suppression of Communism Act—South African law passed in 1951 that stopped all forms of protest against Apartheid.

INDEX

A

Affirmative Action 10, 11, 12, 16
African-Americans In Politics 13, 14, 17, 18, 19
African National Congress (ANC) 33, 34, 35, 36, 38, 39, 41
Afrikaners 32, 33
Apartheid 20, 21, 33, 34, 41
Attica 7, 8, 21

B

Bakke, Allan 11, 12
Bush, George 18, 23, 40
Bush, George W. 23, 42
Busing 9, 10, 21

C

Carter, Jimmy 14
Chisholm, Shirley 13, 21
Clinton, Bill 19

D

de Klerk, F.W. 21, 39, 41
Dinkins, David 17, 18, 40

F

Freedom of Information Act (FOIA) 15

J

Jackson State College 6, 7, 20
Jackson, Jesse 24, 25, 26
Johannesburg, South Africa 32, 33
Johnson, Lyndon B. 10, 11, 20

M

Mandela, Nelson 20, 21, 31, 32, 33, 34, 35, 36, 37, 38, 39, 40, 41
    arrested 35, as leader of ANC 36, captured 37, freed 39, hiding out 36, in America 40, in Pollsmore Prison 38, 39, in Robben Island Prison 37, 38, Nobel Peace Prize 41, opposition to his release 39, 40, organizing resistance 34, protest in Sharpeville Township 35, 36
Mandela, Winnie 35, 38, 41
Marshall, Thurgood 5, 20
Morrison, Toni 21, 26, 27

P

Powell, Colin 21, 22, 23, 42

R

Rainbow Coalition 25
Reagan, Ronald 16, 17
Robben Island Prison 37
Rockefeller, Nelson 8

S

Suppression of Communism Act of 1951 34, 35

W

White flight 6
Winfrey, Oprah 29, 30
Woods, Tiger 27, 28, 29